Home

Poems by
Clementine von Radics

D1247704

Cover designed by Camilo Perdomo
www.camiloperdomo.com

Published in Portland, Oregon,
by Where Are You Press.

For family,
given and chosen

I know now that almost everyone wonders something like that, sooner or later and no matter what he or she is doing, but one of the mixed blessings of being twenty and twenty-one and even twenty-three is the conviction that nothing like this, all evidence to the contrary notwithstanding, has ever happened to anyone before.

—Joan Didion, *Goodbye To All That*

Home

Someday I Will Stop Being Young
And Wanting Stupid Tattoos

There are seven people in my house;
we each have different genders.
I cut my hair over the bathroom sink
and everything I own is dirty.
We sit around the kitchen table
and argue about the compost pile,
and Karl Marx, and the necessity
of violence when The Rev comes.
(whatever the fuck *The Rev* means).

There is a river
running through this city and
every time my best friend laughs
I want to grab him by the shoulders
and shout *Grow old with me*
and never kiss me on the mouth!
I want to spend the next eighty years
together, eating Doritos
and riding bikes.

I want to be Oscar the Grouch.
I want him and his girlfriend

to be Bert and Ernie. We can live

on Sesame Street. I will park
my trashcan on their front stoop
and we can be best friends every day.
If I ever seem grouchy,
I'm just a little afraid of all that fun.

There is a river
running through this city I know
as well as my own name.
It is the first place to ever call
my heart home. It is not poetry
to be in love with the water.
It is not naïve to love what creates
you. It is not blasphemy
to see God in the skyline.

I have built my family
of these buildings and these people.

There is always cold beer
asking to be slurped on back porches.
There are always crushed packs
of American Spirits in my back

pocket. I have been wearing
the same jeans for ten days.

Someday
I will stop being young
and wanting stupid tattoos.

The Three-Day Weekend

I.
If I had a shot of tequila
for every time I swore
I'd never drink again,
I'd be drowning in tequila.
When I get drunk all I do
is talk about you
and kiss boys who aren't you.
Our teeth clacking together;
empty bottles in a trash can.
That is exactly
what's wrong with me.

II.
After the bars close,
we go behind grocery stores,
climb in the dumpsters,
and tear apart the trash bags
like raccoons.
Pawing through the salvageable,
feeling fish heads squish
under our boots.

You find a dozen
half-dead sunflowers
and present them to me
on bended knee.
Here, you say, *Finally,*
something as beautiful
as you are.

III.
The drunk wing of your lips
whispers *baby baby*
as I fall asleep.
We built this crooked house
with our own shaking hands.
We call this place home.

I Am Jealous Of Your Tattoos

And how long
they will stay with you
after I go.

You Have Six Tattoos

Full lips. Good, strong hands.
You have seven freckles
on your back;
they map out the big dipper.

You have a scar on your left arm
you carved there in high school.
The first time you pulled off
your T-shirt, I traced the line
with my fingers, and fell in love
with your strength.

You are a hero for living
from that moment to this one.
You never need to apologize
for how you chose to survive.

Your body is a map
I know every inch of,
and if anyone else
were to kiss me,
all they would taste
is your name.

Things I Do When I Cannot Hold You:

Buy all your favorite foods so I will
be ready when you come home,
because once I did that and you said,
This is how I know you love me.

Go on long walks and think about a
poem my friend wrote that goes
This is how you die by distance.

Hum the sound of the dial tone
under my breath.

Stare at my hands and wonder at
their uses. Think of pawning my
thighs. Consider auctioning off my
hipbones. Place my breasts in a box
on the top shelf of the closet. I do not
need them now.

Roll every story I have to give you
Like a marble on my tongue,
Terrified to choke or swallow them.
Stories like:

Baby, I just found out
pumpkins are technically fruit!
and
Darling! Cary Grant's first job
was in a traveling circus
and
Love, most mammals
are born able to walk
and learn to run within minutes,
so we are not crazy
for moving so fast.

This morning I wrote your name
in the steam on my mirror,
knowing full well it would fade
within minutes.

In my best notebook,
I wrote, *I Miss You I Miss You,*
ten thousand times.

I wrote, *I am definitely missing*
one of my ribs.

I wrote, *I envy the way leaves*
know exactly when to fall
from the branches
and when to come back in the spring.

I wrote, *Everyone else isn't you.*
It turns out that's a huge problem for me.

Bruce Banner Was Not Always
The Hulk

He became that way as the result
of a failed experiment
with a gamma bomb.
Most of us, I think,
have some failure we point to
in our past.

This, we say,
This is why I'm monstrous.

The Hulk does not hulk out
randomly, only when he's stressed
or angry. When Bruce Banner
disappears into the other guy,
he doesn't really care
that he is actually Bruce Banner.
He's just some wild force of nature
that can't control his hands.

When you flashback
to the worst of your memories,
it's like living through death.

Suddenly your kitchen,
the bed, a street corner,
becomes bullets again.
Forever now, you
are at war with a battle
you have already lost.
A body should not be able
to endure that kind of fear
and keep breathing.

The Hulk can't kill himself.
He has tried.
It is so hard to live half-monster,
to hurt everything you love
by trying to protect it wrong.

I keep trying to protect you
from me. From the nights
I don't remember
and all my sickness, my envy,
the days when the shame catches up
and I don't get out of bed at all.
I don't Deal With Things well.

I'm Not Good At Being An Adult.

When I get scared
I can't control my hands,
I would do anything, *anything*
to make myself feel better.

When I calm down,
when I can breathe again,
I am a superhero at the end
of the movie,
when the credits have rolled
and the war is over.
And I have to walk home
through the wreckage of the city
I destroyed
trying to be a savior.

If I am being honest, I know
I can't save you from me.
I can't even save myself.

The thing about the Hulk
is he would give anything

to just be Bruce the scientist.

To be normal,
to never again wake up
naked and lonely,
staring at the destruction
with no one to blame
but herself.

When He Says *You Love Too Deeply*,

Remind him he was warned.

When no one else is awake,
don't call him.

When the poems don't come,
don't open the vodka.

When the poems don't come,
go to sleep.

When you wake up from
the wanting,
go back to sleep.

When he shows up in
your nightmares,
don't offer your forgiveness.

When he offers you his lips,
go for the throat.

When He Asks Me To Describe Fear

I say my mother smelling vodka
on my breath at seventeen.
I say grief is a firework of blue
left on the collarbone. Superheroes
always have broken hearts
and tragic back-stories, so maybe
I'm doing okay. In my dreams,
we are brave enough to leap tall
buildings in a single bound
and see through walls and also
never lie to each other.

Promise me this: when you finally
leave me, you'll get creative.
Tell me I was more disappointing
than your childhood. Send me
your bloody ear with a letter
saying, *I've got to Gogh. You're
making me crazy.* I am hard to love
but know this much:
you are the only thing I like doing
more than writing poems.

I Pity The Woman Who
Will Love You When I Am Done

She will show up to your first date
with a dustpan and broom,
ready to pick up all the pieces
I left you in.
She will hear my name so often
it will begin to dig holes in her. That
is where doubt will grow.
She will look at your neck, your thin
hips, your mouth, wondering
at the ways I touched you.
Offer you her lips, her throat,
the soft pillow of her thighs,
a sacrifice to the altar of virtue.
She will make you
all the promises I did and some
I never could.
She will hear only the terrible stories.
How I left you. How I lied.
She will wonder *(as I have)*
how someone as wonderful as you
could love a sinkhole like the woman
who came before her. Still,

she will compete

with my ghost.
She will understand why
you do not look in the back of closets.
Why you are afraid of every groan
in the cold sweat of night.
She will know
every corner of you
is haunted by me.

Leave Her Lips
For Some Younger, Prettier Girl

They ruby and burn,
stretch full over white teeth; taut
like a drum. I want her
to make music of me, instead
I water plants and envy their wet.
I wash dishes with unsteady hands.

Leave her hands to their work.
They are scarred with stories,
sliding thick down her legs as I stare.
Mouth cotton, thighs pulsing
to the steady rhythm
of her breath.
If I do not play this cool, she
could burn my house down.

Leave my house where it stands.
Let me have this. This crooked
home; the only person
who has ever promised not
to leave me. Let me be worthy
of the first good thing.

I am terrified

I will break his heart
just because I feel restless;
because it is between me
and what I hunger for.

Leave my hunger out of this.
It is stronger than any precaution.
My stomach drops tight
at her voice. My palms itch
for her skin.
When she comes to me,
the closer she gets, the more
I want give.
I want
to give her everything.

I Read Her Palms Naked In Bed

White sheets covering our breasts
and rolling stomachs, shy again
now that the storms of moaning
have passed. I point to her life line,
explain how each crease is a time
she has overcome something.
She laughs, throwing her head back,
letting her hair shake down
her shoulders, exposing
the long column of her throat.
A perfect stretch of canvas.

The warmth of her hand in my hand
is so sweet it makes me dizzy.
I cannot believe her when she says
I am beautiful. She cannot want me,
not the way I want her. My want
is an Empire State Building
I monster-climb with her
clutched in my fist. They make old,
flickering horror movies
about the way I look at her mouth.

It is not a secret
that other women terrify me.

We are always competing in a contest
I don't understand.
I don't know how to beautiful.
I don't know how to gentle.
There is a right way to be this gender.
It has been taught to me
since birth. I have failed every class.

The Brief Two Seconds
After You Ruin Everything

After your grandmother's
wedding ring
slides off your finger
and down the kitchen drain.

After your sister finally
unlocks her mouth. Tells you
what happened the night
you didn't pick up the phone.

After that party
your freshman year of college
when you drank *all the vodka*
and then threw yourself at that boy
who *was so not into you.*

After the picture frames,
the wineglass,
and your vows
lay broken on the floor.

After you drop out of college.

After your mother tells you
not to come home anymore.

After you accept that your father
and the man you love
have the same brown sugar eyes.

After it has been two years,
and you're still not sure
you love him.

After it has been four years,
and you're still not sure
you love him.

After he asks you to marry him,
and you're still not sure
you love him.

After you pull your underwear
from the dark curves
of a stranger's sheets

and leave
without saying good-bye.

After you, sobbing,
confess what you have done,
and he does not forgive you.

There is shame.
There is fear.
And there is this dizzying
freedom.

That Spring Everything Grew Wild
And The Rain Came Down Like
Punishment

I sat on the fire escape
until the ashtrays were snowdrifts,
watching for storms on the horizon.
Begging the world for a reason
to lock all the doors.

Change came to me
so ugly then.
Showed up alone
with moldy suitcases
and too many demands, speaking
the language of hard looks
and wine headaches.
Telling me things I did not want
to know, growling,

*Getting everything you ever wanted
does not make you want less*

and

You break the hearts

of better people
who get in your way.

When will I stop belonging
to this hungry thing inside me?

What no one ever talks about
is how dangerous hope can be.
Call it forgiveness
with teeth.

**You Want To Talk
About The Poems I Wrote For Us**

But those are not words I have
to give you. I am busy still living
in the city where we fell in love.

When you first left, when it was
really bad, I papered the walls of
my bedroom with maps of our

memories. This was not the best
way to forget you. It was better
than drinking alone.

This is a map of downtown. The
black line snakes across the river
from my apartment to your old

house with the dirty kitchen. I
used to chop vegetables while
you stood behind me, wrapped

around me like a ring, singing
Tom Waits in my ear. I miss the

way your breath felt on my neck.

I can't say *I miss you* without
flinching. This is a map of my
old neighborhood.

That red dot is the diner where
we got coffee the first morning
we woke up together. I want a

tattoo of the first morning we
woke up together. I want the
memory to hurt.

This is a map of the river,
running its way through our city.
There is a burn at the center of

the Hawthorne Bridge and you
know why. We don't need to
talk about it.

I am so sorry. I am the worst
kind of brave. I am mad at you
because these days being mad

is as close as I get to kissing
your forehead. It keeps rain-
ing but nothing looks cleaner.

Everything in Portland
is a postcard saying
Wish You Were Here!

So many of the books
in my bedroom
used to be your books.

The Story Behind Lobsters

Is that they weren't considered
a delicacy until the 19th century.
Before that they were peasant food,
most often served in prisons.

The story behind diamonds
is they were just rocks until 1938
when a marketing campaign
forever linked them with love.

The story behind us
is you said *I won't wait forever,*
and with an arrogance reserved
for those who have never known
loss, I did not listen.

The story behind art
is that it is never a masterpiece
until it has been bought and hung
on the wall in someone
else's home.

The story behind us

is until I lost you

I had no idea
what you were worth.

The World Is Very Simple
When The World Is Just You
And Me In Bed Together

You trace the curves of my body
like they are so new to you.
Like you haven't been learning
my legs for months.

I kiss your forehead
like you are a child
because I am good with children
and that is how I know
to comfort.

You kiss up my neck
as I tell you about the bruise
on my knee.
baby baby, you say,
as often as you draw breath.
You kiss down my stomach
as I sigh in time
with the birds outside.

You tell me it's strange

we're grown-ups.

I say you and I
have too many freckles and bruises
to be real grown-ups.
I say when I finally grow up
I'm gonna write poems
that aren't love poems and
I will have lots and lots of children
and they will be small
and beautiful and I will always
kiss them on the forehead.

You kiss me
with your whole body.
You kiss me so much
it bends my spine backward.
I think even if
you are mostly flaws and sad stories,
so am I and so is everyone.
I think your flaws and sad stories
go well with mine.
I promise to call your sad stories
baby baby and kiss them

in time with the birds outside.
I tell you all that,

and you say *it's too early*.
You call me *baby*.

Some Things You Could Do To Heal Yourself:

Don't kiss the boy with no bicycle.
Don't kiss the girl with moon lips.
Don't kiss wild animals
or hand grenades.
You fuck for the same reasons
lost men drink.
Stop.

Don't spend another day
mourning the smell of her shampoo.

You silly little girl,
you think you've survived so long
survival shouldn't hurt anymore.
You keep trying to turn
your body bulletproof.
You keep trying to turn your heart
bomb shelter. Stop, darling.
You are soft and alive. You bruise
and heal. Cherish it.
It is what you are born to do.

It will not be beautiful, but the truth

never is. Come now,
you promised yourself.
You promised
you'd live through this.

Out East Beyond The City It's Quiet

And the rain-soaked porch
still feels like your lips
on my forehead.

In the living room,
Johnny Cash is groaning again
about the beer he had
for breakfast.

The beer I had for breakfast
just punched its way
out of my mouth. The sun
is squinting at my bad decisions.

I'm trying to dry out,
but I'm worried my hands
will shake too hard to write.
I'm worried I will earthquake
from my body.

I wonder what you'd think
if you saw me now.

If you read this,
I'm doing just fine.
I'm still a sheep in wolf's clothing.
I'm still struggling with all
the old questions.

I'd still give anything
to hear you call me *Darlin'*.

If you read this
and you're thinking of me,
I am thinking of you too.

All That's Left To Tell:

I.
When I was trying
to quit smoking
and we drank white wine
from Mason jars,
you called my freckles
cocoa powder
and I called your green eyes
celery.

II.
I am learning how
to be a grown-up
who pays bills,
cooks her own meals,
and doesn't cry at words like
I think I just want to be friends.

III.
The truth is this:
Love is an organic thing.
It rots and softens.

**It Is All Loneliness,
The Way You Live**

You get up. Make the bed
like you are trying to prove
a point. You make coffee
that is never quite right
and never finish it.

This is the third day
you've worn this dress.
Eventually, you will paint
your nails again; wash
the grease from your hair.
Once you have someone
besides your own reflection
to impress.

You spend more hours
not writing poems about him
than you do dancing.
Go to parties where you know
you will only stay an hour.
Lean quietly against the wall,
watching people rich

with easy laughter.

Your smile is a cracked boat
in a flooded river. Close,
but still useless.

You do not talk to strangers —
just stand there. A begging dog
below the dinner table,
with eyes that say,
Please, come, be my friend.
I am a coward, but I'm hungry.

When I Was Seven Years Old

We adopted a dog
who ran away two weeks later,
back to the home of the man
who didn't want her.

We found her there,
howling at the darkened windows.
No one lived there anymore.
All the doors were locked. Dogs
are so disappointing in their loyalty
to the wrong things.

When Oscar Wilde was asked
about the man he went to prison
for loving too publicly, he said,
He ruined my life,
for that very reason I seem forced
to love him more.

And I imagine that
being the mother of a serial killer
is like being a child
with only broken dolls left

to play with.

All of this is to say
I'm having the kind of afternoon
where I break a dish
and stand over the kitchen sink
for hours, staring
at the two irreparable halves.

There is no longer
a woman in my body.
Just this screaming child
who does not listen.
She only wants.
And wants. And wants.
Stubborn in her devotion.

And he is still gone.
And grief is a swamp that sinks
much deeper than you'd expect.

And I am still here.
I still remember him.

The Poet Finally Drops The Bullshit:

I am 15 and he is my first boyfriend.
He is 18 and 6' 4" and his hands are
the size of thick textbooks. He says he
has a lot to teach me. He is drowning
in his own sadness. Drowning people
often believe that if they grab hold of
someone else they can be saved, but it
just makes you both sink faster.

I am 17 and she is my first girlfriend.
The only thing we do more than fight
is fuck each other. I tell her about the
boy's hands and she tries to stretch
her fingers wide to mimic them. I say,
Stop it. I say, *I love you as you are.*

I am 19 and in the first of many dirty
rooms with books strewn everywhere
and a mattress in one corner. These
rooms always belong to boys with
unshaved faces and tender hearts.

Boys like this are a dime a dozen, but
I don't know that yet because tonight
I'm with the first one. He hands me
a beer. He says he thinks I'm smart.
He orders me to take off my clothes.

I am 20 and in love with someone
who lies. The punishment for telling
lies is being cruel. The punishment
for being cruel is being abandoned.

I am 21 and it is not sex because I did
not say yes. I say stop but that does
not make it stop. I am 22 and crying
because this new set of promises
wants to kiss me, and I still taste like
betrayal.

She Sits Me Down

On her worn pink couch
and says there has to be
some root to this.

I tell her, *I don't know.*
I don't know.

But every time a man yells
I am seven years old again
and he is packing that suitcase
once more.

Picking me up by the neck,
teaching me obedience. To be soft,
like the belly of a fish
exposed to a knife.

All This Time

I drank you like the cure,
when maybe
you were the poison.

Something is wrong.
There are flies over the bed.
Everything smells
like wasted fruit.

And She Says

I can't help you
if you keep making up stories.

Sit up on the couch.
Look me in the eye.

It is time to be honest.

It's Just So Strange

He used to love me,
and now
he's just a stranger
who happens to know
all my secrets.

My Father Sits Me Down
To Teach Me How
To Play Guitar

First off, he tells me, your fingers are
going to blister. Your fingers are
going to bleed.

Here: Let's start with the D chord.
This is how you play *Down On The
Bayou*. Vibrations travel through
the body, and that is how sound
is made.

Here: This is how I pray. These are
the notes that roughly translate to
Hallelujah. This is how you play *I
Won't Back Down*. Now, Don't Back
Down.

Every song has a rhythm you have
to find like a pulse. The beauty of
music is you are never done learning.
There is always time for you to get
better.

Clementine, you have to push harder
with your fingers! You have to be
stronger about this.

Here: This how I mourn. How I take
revenge and tell stories, ask the
woman you love to dance with you.
This how I built our family. This is
how you built our home.

Here: This is the heartbeat
of the song you were named for.
Have I ever told you
why your name is Clementine?

The first time I held you
all I could think was,
Oh my darlin', Oh my darlin'.

Oh my darlin', It is time you learn
everything worth loving takes hard
work and patience.

I know you. You are the good half
of me. People like us are not good
with words. What we mean
gets muddled and wrong somewhere
between our minds and our mouths.

We make art to say how we feel.
Here: these are the chords to *Make
You Feel My Love.*

**Cleopatra's Palace
As An Elaborate Metaphor
For Why I Didn't Call Him Back:**

I.
When I think of love, I
think of a snakebite
to the chest.

II.
He was right.
Uncountable lifetimes ago
there was an empire in Egypt.
But we burned the libraries.
We destroyed the temples.
Everything that was beautiful then
is lost to us now.

III.
These days poetry
is the only language
I know how to speak.
But he speaks anthropology.
He speaks hieroglyphs. He
spends his life studying things

I can only bury in metaphors.

IV.
My body
is a war-weathered monument
to the desert.

V.
My chest
is the stone tomb
inside it.

VI.
Our vows,
a book of prayers I buried
with the dead.

VII.
Last year they found
Cleopatra's palace sunk deep
in the Mediterranean Sea.
They are going to build
a museum.

You and I both know
anything they could learn
from the ruins
of her once home
is not worth
emptying oceans for.

The First Time
You Washed Up At Our Door

After a night
of out-swimming your own ghosts,
I was seven years old.
You smelled like something sour.
The jagged, bleeding zipper
of your mouth
made you look
like a Halloween mask.

You healed beautifully, swore
you were dry. Lasted
30 days and showed up again,
spilling over our porch,
sobriety chips still jangling
in your pocket.

Each year that passed
has brought you a new set of scars
until you don't even look
like a man anymore.
More like a warning. A car
wrapped around a telephone pole,

an animal limping along

the edge of the highway.
The lighthouse, its huge, single eye
warning of storms,
screaming, *Turn around, go.*
There is no harbor here.

Tonight you are in a hospital
somewhere south of me. A machine
is forcing life into a heart
you have been trying to drown
my whole life.

I am sorry I haven't visited.
I know I haven't called.
I don't know why this business
of living is so much harder
for you.

This morning
I saw a bottle thrown
out of a car. The glass shattered
in a dangerous, glittering
explosion. Staining the grit

and the cracks of the sidewalk,

a mosaic of beautiful, senseless
destruction.

I Stopped Going To Therapy

Because I knew my therapist
was right, and I wanted
to keep being wrong.
I wanted to wear my bad habits
like charms on a bracelet.
I did not want to be brave.
I think I like my brain best
in a bar fight with my heart.
I think I like myself a little broken.
I'm okay if that makes me
harder to love. I like poetry
better than therapy anyway.
The poems never judge me
for healing wrong.

This Is How We Lose Ourselves

In trees and artichoke flowers.
Long hours spent near the river,
letting her flirt with our legs,
each lap against the rocks
whispering,
Jump in, disturb me, eventually
the waves will still and you
will belong here
as much as the fish do.

We are not in love.
Not the way I've been told
being in love feels like.
But we have been sleeping
beside each other
for so many nights, and I
am the most beautiful doormat
you have ever walked over.

This is how we lose ourselves.
Early mornings picking blackberries,
knees and hands always dirty
from bicycle accidents,
bruised and bleeding.

Most days we feel more alive
than anyone has ever been.
Most days we feel terrified.

Acknowledgments

"Bruce" (The Hulk Poem) is after a poem by Doc Luben.

"The Poet Finally Drops The Bullshit" was first published in *Whiskey Paper*.

About the Author

Clementine von Radics likes reading palms and getting friendship tattoos. She is the author of *As Often As Miracles* and the founder of Where Are You Press. She lives in Portland, Oregon.

Also From Where Are You Press

Healing Old Wounds With New Stiches
Meggie Royer

As Often As Miracles
Clementine von Radics

It Looked A Lot Like Love
Kristina Haynes

Until I Learned What It Meant
Yena Sharma Purmasir

Where Are You Press prints and publishes 3-5 young, talented authors every year. We are based in Portland, Oregon.